Chapter 1: Introduction to the x86 about our OS

What is the x86 architecture?

> The term x86 denotes a family of backward compatible instruction set architectures based on the Intel 8086 CPU.

The x86 architecture is the most common instruction set architecture since its introduction in 1981 for the IBM PC. A large amount of software, including operating systems (OS's) such as DOS, Windows, Linux, BSD, Solaris and Mac OS X, function with x86-based hardware.

In this course we are not going to design an operating system for the x86-64 architecture but for x86-32, thanks to backward compatibility, our OS will be compatible with our newer PCs (but take caution if you want to test it on your real machine).

Our Operating System

The goal is to build a very simple UNIX-based operating system in C++, but the goal is not to just build a "proof-of-concept". The OS should be able to boot, start a userland shell and be extensible.

The OS will be built for the x86 architecture, running on 32 bits, and compatible with IBM PCs.

Specifications:

* Code in C++
* x86, 32 bit architecture
* Boot with Grub
* Kind of modular system for drivers
* Kind of UNIX style
* Multitasking
* ELF executable in userland
* Modules (accessible in userland using /dev/...) :
    * IDE disks
    * DOS partitions
    * Clock
    * EXT2 (read only)
    * Boch VBE
* Userland :

* API Posix
* LibC
* "Can" run a shell or some executables like Lua,
...

Chapter 2: Setup the development environment

The first step is to setup a good and viable development environment. Using Vagrant and Virtualbox, you'll be able to compile and test your OS from all the OSs (Linux, Windows or Mac).

Install Vagrant

> Vagrant is free and open-source software for creating and configuring virtual development environments. It can be considered a wrapper around VirtualBox.

Vagrant will help us create a clean virtual development environment on whatever system you are using.
The first step is to download and install Vagrant for your system at http://www.vagrantup.com/.

Install Virtualbox

> Oracle VM VirtualBox is a virtualization software package for x86 and AMD64/Intel64-based computers.

Vagrant needs Virtualbox to work, Download and install for your system at https://www.virtualbox.org/wiki/Downloads.

Start and test your development environment

Once Vagrant and Virtualbox are installed, you need to download the ubuntu lucid32 image for Vagrant:

```
vagrant box add lucid32
http://files.vagrantup.com/lucid32.box
```

Once the lucid32 image is ready, we need to define our development environment using a *Vagrantfile*, [create a file named
Vagrantfile](https://github.com/SamyPesse/How-to-Make-a-Computer-Operating-
System/blob/master/src/Vagrantfile). This file defines

what prerequisites our environment needs: nasm, make, build-essential, grub and qemu.

Start your box using:

```
vagrant up
```

You can now access your box by using ssh to connect to the virtual box using:

```
vagrant ssh
```

The code will be available in the */vagrant* directory:

```
cd /vagrant
```

Build and test our operating system

The file [**Makefile**](https://github.com/SamyPesse/How-to-Make-a-Computer-Operating-System/blob/master/src/Makefile) defines some basics rules for building the kernel, the user libc and some userland programs.

Build:

```
make all
```

Test our operating system with qemu:

```
make run
```

The documentation for qemu is available at [QEMU Emulator Documentation](http://wiki.qemu.org/download/qemu-doc.html).

You can exit the emulator using: \<Ctrl-a x\>.
■■

Chapter 3: First boot with GRUB

How the boot works?

When an x86-based computer is turned on, it begins a
complex path to get to the stage where control is
transferred to our kernel's "main" routine (`kmain()`).
For this course, we are only going to consider the BIOS
boot method and not it's successor (UEFI).

The BIOS boot sequence is: RAM detection -> Hardware
detection/Initialization -> Boot sequence.

The most important step for us is the "Boot sequence",
where the BIOS is done with its initialization and
tries to transfer control to the next stage of the
bootloader process.

During the "Boot sequence", the BIOS will try to
determine a "boot device" (e.g. floppy disk, hard-disk,
CD, USB flash memory device or network). Our Operating
System will initially boot from the hard-disk (but it
will be possible to boot it from a CD or a USB flash
memory device in future). A device is considered
bootable if the bootsector contains the valid signature
bytes `0x55` and `0xAA` at sectors 511 and 512
respectively.

BIOS physically searches for a boot device by loading
the first 512 bytes from the bootsector of each device
into physical memory, starting at the address `0x7C00`
(1 KiB below the 32 KiB mark). When the valid signature
bytes are detected, BIOS transfers control to the
`0x7C00` memory address (via a jump instruction) in
order to execute the bootsector code.

Throughout this process the CPU has been running in 16-
bit Real Mode (the default state for x86 CPUs in order
to maintain backwards compatibility). To execute the
32-bit instructions within our kernel, a bootloader is
required to switch the CPU into Protected Mode.

What is GRUB?

> GNU GRUB (short for GNU GRand Unified Bootloader) is a boot loader package from the GNU Project. GRUB is the reference implementation of the Free Software Foundation's Multiboot Specification, which provides a user the choice to boot one of multiple operating systems installed on a computer or select a specific kernel configuration available on a particular operating system's partitions.

To make it simple, GRUB is the first thing booted by the machine (a boot-loader) and will simplify the loading of our kernel stored on the hard-disk.

Why are we using GRUB?

* GRUB is very simple to use
* Make it very simple to load 32bits kernels without needs of 16bits code
* Multiboot with Linux, Windows and others
* Make it easy to load external modules in memory

How to use GRUB?

GRUB uses the Multiboot specification, the executable binary should be 32bits and must contain a special header (multiboot header) in its 8192 first bytes. Our kernel will be a ELF executable file ("Executable and Linkable Format", a common standard file format for executables in most UNIX system).

The first boot sequence of our kernel is written in Assembly: [start.asm](https://github.com/SamyPesse/How-to-Make-a-Computer-Operating-System/blob/master/src/kernel/arch/x86/start.asm) and we use a linker file to define our executable structure: [linker.ld](https://github.com/SamyPesse/How-to-Make-a-Computer-Operating-System/blob/master/src/kernel/arch/x86/linker.ld).

This boot process also initializes some of our C++ runtime, it will be described in the next chapter.

Multiboot header structure:

```
```

```
struct multiboot_info {
        u32 flags;
        u32 low_mem;
        u32 high_mem;
        u32 boot_device;
        u32 cmdline;
        u32 mods_count;
        u32 mods_addr;
        struct {
                u32 num;
                u32 size;
                u32 addr;
                u32 shndx;
        } elf_sec;
        unsigned long mmap_length;
        unsigned long mmap_addr;
        unsigned long drives_length;
        unsigned long drives_addr;
        unsigned long config_table;
        unsigned long boot_loader_name;
        unsigned long apm_table;
        unsigned long vbe_control_info;
        unsigned long vbe_mode_info;
        unsigned long vbe_mode;
        unsigned long vbe_interface_seg;
        unsigned long vbe_interface_off;
        unsigned long vbe_interface_len;
};
```

You can use the command ```mbchk kernel.elf``` to validate your kernel.elf file against the multiboot standard. You can also use the command ```nm -n kernel.elf``` to validate the offset of the different objects in the ELF binary.

Create a disk image for our kernel and grub

The script [diskimage.sh](https://github.com/SamyPesse/How-to-Make-a-Computer-Operating-System/blob/master/src/sdk/diskimage.sh) will generate a hard disk image than can be used by QEMU.

The first step is to create a hard-disk image (c.img) using qemu-img:

```
qemu-img create c.img 2M
```

We need now to partition the disk using fdisk:

```
fdisk ./c.img

# Switch to Expert commands
> x

# Change number of cylinders (1-1048576)
> c
> 4

# Change number of heads (1-256, default 16):
> h
> 16

# Change number of sectors/track (1-63, default 63)
> s
> 63

# Return to main menu
> r

# Add a new partition
> n

# Choose primary partition
> p

# Choose partition number
> 1

# Choose first cylinder (1-4, default 1)
> 1

# Choose last cylinder, +cylinders or +size{K,M,G} (1-
4, default 4)
> 4

# Toggle bootable flag
> a

# Choose first partition for bootable flag
```

> 1

```
# Write table to disk and exit
> w
```

We need now to attach the created partition to the loop-device (which allows a file to be access like a block device) using losetup. The offset of the partition is passed as an argument and calculated using: **offset= start_sector * bytes_by_sector**.

Using ```fdisk -l -u c.img```, you get: 63 * 512 = 32356.

```
losetup -o 32256 /dev/loop1 ./c.img
```

We create a EXT2 filesystem on this new device using:

```
mke2fs /dev/loop1
```

We copy our files on a mounted disk:

```
mount  /dev/loop1 /mnt/
cp -R bootdisk/* /mnt/
umount /mnt/
```

Install GRUB on the disk:

```
grub --device-map=/dev/null << EOF
device (hd0) ./c.img
geometry (hd0) 4 16 63
root (hd0,0)
setup (hd0)
quit
EOF
```

And finally we detach the loop device:

```
losetup -d /dev/loop1
```

See Also

* [GNU GRUB on
Wikipedia](http://en.wikipedia.org/wiki/GNU_GRUB)
* [Multiboot
specification](https://www.gnu.org/software/grub/manual
/multiboot/multiboot.html)

■■■

Chapter 4: Backbone of the OS and C++ runtime

C++ kernel run-time

A kernel can be programmed in C++, it is very similar
to making a kernel in C, except that there are a few
pitfalls you must take into account (runtime support,
constructors, ...)

The compiler will assume that all the necessary C++
runtime support is available by default, but as we are
not linking in libsupc++ into your C++ kernel, we need
to add some basic functions that can be found in the
[cxx.cc](https://github.com/SamyPesse/How-to-Make-a-
Computer-Operating-
System/blob/master/src/kernel/runtime/cxx.cc) file.

Caution: The operators `new` and `delete` cannot be
used before virtual memory and pagination have been
initialized.

Basic C/C++ functions

The kernel code can't use functions from the standard
libraries so we need to add some basic functions for
managing memory and strings:

```cpp
void    itoa(char *buf, unsigned long int n, int base);

void *  memset(char *dst,char src, int n);
void *  memcpy(char *dst, char *src, int n);

int     strlen(char *s);
```

```
int     strcmp(const char *dst, char *src);
int     strcpy(char *dst,const char *src);
void    strcat(void *dest,const void *src);
char *  strncpy(char *destString, const char
*sourceString,int maxLength);
int     strncmp( const char* s1, const char* s2, int c
);
```

These functions are defined in
[string.cc](https://github.com/SamyPesse/How-to-Make-a-
Computer-Operating-
System/blob/master/src/kernel/runtime/string.cc),
[memory.cc](https://github.com/SamyPesse/How-to-Make-a-
Computer-Operating-
System/blob/master/src/kernel/runtime/memory.cc),
[itoa.cc](https://github.com/SamyPesse/How-to-Make-a-
Computer-Operating-
System/blob/master/src/kernel/runtime/itoa.cc)

C types

During the next step, we are going to use different
types in our code, most of the types we are going to
use unsigned types (all the bits are used to stored the
integer, in signed types one bit is used to signal the
sign):

```cpp
typedef unsigned char   u8;
typedef unsigned short         u16;
typedef unsigned int    u32;
typedef unsigned long long     u64;

typedef signed char     s8;
typedef signed short    s16;
typedef signed int             s32;
typedef signed long long       s64;
```

Compile our kernel

Compiling a kernel is not the same thing as compiling a
linux executable, we can't use a standard library and
should have no dependencies to the system.

Our [Makefile](https://github.com/SamyPesse/How-to-Make-a-Computer-Operating-System/blob/master/src/kernel/Makefile) will define the process to compile and link our kernel.

For x86 architecture, the followings arguments will be used for gcc/g++/ld:

```
# Linker
LD=ld
LDFLAG= -melf_i386 -static  -L ./  -T ./arch/$(ARCH)/linker.ld

# C++ compiler
SC=g++
FLAG= $(INCDIR) -g -O2 -w -trigraphs -fno-builtin  -fno-exceptions -fno-stack-protector -O0 -m32  -fno-rtti -nostdlib -nodefaultlibs

# Assembly compiler
ASM=nasm
ASMFLAG=-f elf -o
```

Chapter 5: Base classes for managing x86 architecture

Now that we know how to compile our C++ kernel and boot the binary using GRUB, we can start to do some cool things in C/C++.

Printing to the screen console

We are going to use VGA default mode (03h) to display some text to the user. The screen can be directly accessed using the video memory at 0xB8000. The screen resolution is 80x25 and each character on the screen is defined by 2 bytes: one for the character code, and one for the style flag. This means that the total size of the video memory is 4000B (80B*25B*2B).

In the IO class ([io.cc](https://github.com/SamyPesse/How-to-Make-a-Computer-Operating-System/blob/master/src/kernel/arch/x86/io.cc)),:
* **x,y**: define the cursor position on the screen
* **real_screen**: define the video memory pointer

* **putc(char c)**: print a unique character on the
screen and manage cursor position
* **printf(char* s, ...)**: print a string

We add a method **putc** to the [IO
Class](https://github.com/SamyPesse/How-to-Make-a-
Computer-Operating-
System/blob/master/src/kernel/arch/x86/io.cc) to put a
character on the screen and update the (x,y) position.

```cpp
/* put a byte on screen */
void Io::putc(char c){
        kattr = 0x07;
        unsigned char *video;
        video = (unsigned char *) (real_screen+ 2 * x +
160 * y);
        // newline
        if (c == '\n') {
                x = 0;
                y++;
        // back space
        } else if (c == '\b') {
                if (x) {
                        *(video + 1) = 0x0;
                        x--;
                }
        // horizontal tab
        } else if (c == '\t') {
                x = x + 8 - (x % 8);
        // carriage return
        } else if (c == '\r') {
                x = 0;
        } else {
                *video = c;
                *(video + 1) = kattr;

                x++;
                if (x > 79) {
                        x = 0;
                        y++;
                }
        }
        if (y > 24)
                scrollup(y - 24);
}
```

We also add a useful and very known method:
[printf](https://github.com/SamyPesse/How-to-Make-a-Computer-Operating-System/blob/master/src/kernel/arch/x86/io.cc#L155)

```cpp
/* put a string in screen */
void Io::print(const char *s, ...){
        va_list ap;

        char buf[16];
        int i, j, size, buflen, neg;

        unsigned char c;
        int ival;
        unsigned int uival;

        va_start(ap, s);

        while ((c = *s++)) {
                size = 0;
                neg = 0;

                if (c == 0)
                        break;
                else if (c == '%') {
                        c = *s++;
                        if (c >= '0' && c <= '9') {
                                size = c - '0';
                                c = *s++;
                        }

                        if (c == 'd') {
                                ival = va_arg(ap, int);
                                if (ival < 0) {
                                        uival = 0 - ival;
                                        neg++;
                                } else
                                        uival = ival;
                                itoa(buf, uival, 10);

                                buflen = strlen(buf);
                                if (buflen < size)
                                        for (i = size, j
= buflen; i >= 0;
                                             i--, j--)
```

```c
                                    buf[i] =
                                        (j >=
                                        0) ?
buf[j] : '0';

                    if (neg)
                        print("-%s",
buf);
                    else
                        print(buf);
            }
          else if (c == 'u') {
                uival = va_arg(ap, int);
                itoa(buf, uival, 10);

                buflen = strlen(buf);
                if (buflen < size)
                        for (i = size, j
= buflen; i >= 0;

                                i--, j--)
                                    buf[i] =
                                        (j >=
                                        0) ?
buf[j] : '0';

                print(buf);
            } else if (c == 'x' || c == 'X')
{

                uival = va_arg(ap, int);
                itoa(buf, uival, 16);

                buflen = strlen(buf);
                if (buflen < size)
                        for (i = size, j
= buflen; i >= 0;

                                i--, j--)
                                    buf[i] =
                                        (j >=
                                        0) ?
buf[j] : '0';

                print("0x%s", buf);
            } else if (c == 'p') {
                uival = va_arg(ap, int);
                itoa(buf, uival, 16);
                size = 8;
```

```
                                      buflen = strlen(buf);
                                      if (buflen < size)
                                             for (i = size, j
= buflen; i >= 0;
                                                 i--, j--)
                                                    buf[i] =
                                                          (j >=
                                                          0) ?
buf[j] : '0';

                                      print("0x%s", buf);
                          } else if (c == 's') {
                                      print((char *)
va_arg(ap, int));
                          }
                    } else
                          putc(c);
          }

          return;
}
```

Assembly interface

A large number of instructions are available in
Assembly but there is not equivalent in C (like cli,
sti, in and out), so we need an interface to these
instructions.

In C, we can include Assembly using the directive
"asm()", gcc use gas to compile the assembly.

Caution: gas use the AT&T syntax.

```cpp
/* output byte */
void Io::outb(u32 ad, u8 v){
      asmv("outb %%al, %%dx" :: "d" (ad), "a" (v));;
}
/* output word */
void Io::outw(u32 ad, u16 v){
      asmv("outw %%ax, %%dx" :: "d" (ad), "a" (v));
}
/* output word */
void Io::outl(u32 ad, u32 v){
      asmv("outl %%eax, %%dx" : : "d" (ad), "a" (v));
```

```
}
/* input byte */
u8 Io::inb(u32 ad){
        u8 _v;          \
        asmv("inb %%dx, %%al" : "=a" (_v) : "d" (ad));
\
        return _v;
}
/* input word */
u16     Io::inw(u32 ad){
        u16 _v;                 \
        asmv("inw %%dx, %%ax" : "=a" (_v) : "d" (ad));
        return _v;
}
/* input word */
u32     Io::inl(u32 ad){
        u32 _v;                 \
        asmv("inl %%dx, %%eax" : "=a" (_v) : "d" (ad));
        return _v;
}
```

Chapter 6: GDT

Thanks to GRUB, your kernel is no longer in real-mode,
but already in [protected
mode](http://en.wikipedia.org/wiki/Protected_mode),
this mode allows us to use all the possibilities of the
microprocessor such as virtual memory management,
paging and safe multi-tasking.

What is the GDT?

The
[GDT](http://en.wikipedia.org/wiki/Global_Descriptor_Ta
ble) ("Global Descriptor Table") is a data structure
used to define the different memory areas: the base
address, the size and access privileges like execute
and write. These memory areas are called "segments".

We are going to use the GDT to define different memory
segments:

* *"code"*: kernel code, used to stored the executable
binary code
* *"data"*: kernel data
* *"stack"*: kernel stack, used to stored the call
stack during kernel execution

* *"ucode"*: user code, used to stored the executable
binary code for user program
* *"udata"*: user program data
* *"ustack"*: user stack, used to stored the call stack
during execution in userland

How to load our GDT?

GRUB initializes a GDT but this GDT is does not
correspond to our kernel.
The GDT is loaded using the LGDT assembly instruction.
It expects the location of a GDT description structure:

![GDTR](./gdtr.png)

And the C structure:

```cpp
struct gdtr {
        u16 limite;
        u32 base;
} __attribute__ ((packed));
```

Caution: the directive ```__attribute__
((packed))``` signal to gcc that the structure should
use as little memory as possible. Without this
directive, gcc include some bytes to optimize the
memory alignment and the access during execution.

Now we need to define our GDT table and then load it
using LGDT. The GDT table can be stored wherever we
want in memory, its address should just be signaled to
the process using the GDTR registry.

The GDT table is composed of segments with the
following structure:

![GDTR](./gdtentry.png)

And the C structure:

```cpp
struct gdtdesc {
        u16 lim0_15;
        u16 base0_15;
        u8 base16_23;
```

```cpp
        u8 acces;
        u8 lim16_19:4;
        u8 other:4;
        u8 base24_31;
} __attribute__ ((packed));
```

How to define our GDT table?

We need now to define our GDT in memory and finally
load it using the GDTR registry.

We are going to store our GDT at the address:

```cpp
#define GDTBASE 0x00000800
```

The function **init_gdt_desc** in
[x86.cc](https://github.com/SamyPesse/How-to-Make-a-
Computer-Operating-
System/blob/master/src/kernel/arch/x86/x86.cc)
initialize a gdt segment descriptor.

```cpp
void init_gdt_desc(u32 base, u32 limite, u8 acces, u8
other, struct gdtdesc *desc)
{
        desc->lim0_15 = (limite & 0xffff);
        desc->base0_15 = (base & 0xffff);
        desc->base16_23 = (base & 0xff0000) >> 16;
        desc->acces = acces;
        desc->lim16_19 = (limite & 0xf0000) >> 16;
        desc->other = (other & 0xf);
        desc->base24_31 = (base & 0xff000000) >> 24;
        return;
}
```

And the function **init_gdt** initialize the GDT, some
parts of the below function will be explained later and
are used for multitasking.

```cpp
void init_gdt(void)
{
        default_tss.debug_flag = 0x00;
```

```c
        default_tss.io_map = 0x00;
        default_tss.esp0 = 0x1FFF0;
        default_tss.ss0 = 0x18;

        /* initialize gdt segments */
        init_gdt_desc(0x0, 0x0, 0x0, 0x0, &kgdt[0]);
        init_gdt_desc(0x0, 0xFFFFF, 0x9B, 0x0D,
&kgdt[1]);       /* code */
        init_gdt_desc(0x0, 0xFFFFF, 0x93, 0x0D,
&kgdt[2]);       /* data */
        init_gdt_desc(0x0, 0x0, 0x97, 0x0D, &kgdt[3]);

        init_gdt_desc(0x0, 0xFFFFF, 0xFF, 0x0D,
&kgdt[4]);       /* ucode */
        init_gdt_desc(0x0, 0xFFFFF, 0xF3, 0x0D,
&kgdt[5]);       /* udata */
        init_gdt_desc(0x0, 0x0, 0xF7, 0x0D, &kgdt[6]);

        init_gdt_desc((u32) & default_tss, 0x67, 0xE9,
0x00, &kgdt[7]);        /* descripteur de tss */

        /* initialize the gdtr structure */
        kgdtr.limite = GDTSIZE * 8;
        kgdtr.base = GDTBASE;

        /* copy the gdtr to its memory area */
        memcpy((char *) kgdtr.base, (char *) kgdt,
kgdtr.limite);

        /* load the gdtr registry */
        asm("lgdtl (kgdtr)");

        /* initiliaz the segments */
        asm("   movw $0x10, %ax        \n \
            movw %ax, %ds       \n \
            movw %ax, %es       \n \
            movw %ax, %fs       \n \
            movw %ax, %gs       \n \
            ljmp $0x08, $next \n \
            next:               \n");
}
```
```
```

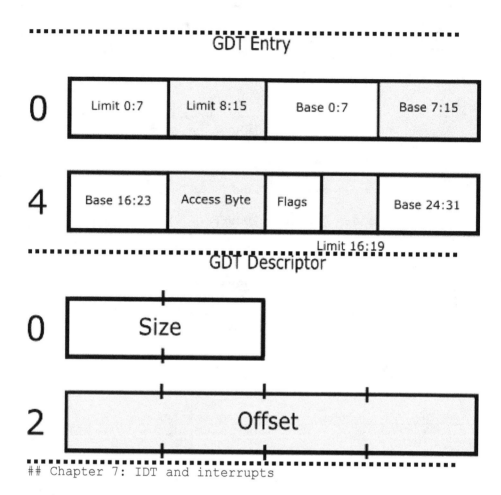

Chapter 7: IDT and interrupts

An interrupt is a signal to the processor emitted by hardware or software indicating an event that needs immediate attention.

There are 3 types of interrupts:

- **Hardware interrupts:** are sent to the processor from an external device (keyboard, mouse, hard disk, ...). Hardware interrupts were introduced as a way to reduce wasting the processor's valuable time in polling loops, waiting for external events.
- **Software interrupts:** are initiated voluntarily by the software. It's used to manage system calls.
- **Exceptions:** are used for errors or events occurring during program execution that are exceptional enough that they cannot be handled within the program itself (division by zero, page fault, ...)

The keyboard example:

When the user pressed a key on the keyboard, the keyboard controller will signal an interrupt to the Interrupt Controller. If the interrupt is not masked, the controller signal the interrupt to the processor, the processor will execute a routine to manage the interrupt (key pressed or key released), this routine could for example get the pressed key from the keyboard controller and print the key to the screen. Once the character processing routine is completed, the interrupted job can be resumed.

What is the PIC?

The [PIC](http://en.wikipedia.org/wiki/Programmable_Interrupt_Controller) (Programmable interrupt controller)is a device that is used to combine several sources of interrupt onto one or more CPU lines, while allowing priority levels to be assigned to its interrupt outputs. When the device has multiple interrupt outputs to assert, it asserts them in the order of their relative priority.

The best known PIC is the 8259A, each 8259A can handle 8 devices but most computers have two controllers: one master and one slave, it's allow the computer to manager interrupts from 14 devices.

In this chapter, we will need to program this controller to initialize it and mask interrupts.

What is the IDT?

> The Interrupt Descriptor Table (IDT) is a data structure used by the x86 architecture to implement an interrupt vector table. The IDT is used by the processor to determine the correct response to interrupts and exceptions.

Our kernel is going to use the IDT to define the different functions to be executed when an interrupt occurred.

Like the GDT, the IDT is loaded using the LIDTL
assembly instruction. It expects the location of a IDT
description structure:

```cpp
struct idtr {
        u16 limite;
        u32 base;
} __attribute__ ((packed));
```

The IDT table is composed of IDT segments with the
following structure:

```cpp
struct idtdesc {
        u16 offset0_15;
        u16 select;
        u16 type;
        u16 offset16_31;
} __attribute__ ((packed));
```

Caution: the directive ```__attribute__
((packed))``` signal to gcc that the structure should
use as little memory as possible. Without this
directive, gcc include some bytes to optimize the
memory alignment and the access during execution.

Now we need to define our IDT table and then load it
using LIDTL. The IDT table can be stored wherever we
want in memory, its address should just be signaled to
the process using the IDTR registry.

Here is a table of common interrupts (Maskable hardware
interrupt are called IRQ):

IRQ	Description
0	Programmable Interrupt Timer Interrupt
1	Keyboard Interrupt
2	Cascade (used internally by the two PICs. never raised)
3	COM2 (if enabled)
4	COM1 (if enabled)
5	LPT2 (if enabled)

6	Floppy Disk
7	LPT1
8	CMOS real-time clock (if enabled)
9	Free for peripherals / legacy SCSI / NIC
10	Free for peripherals / SCSI / NIC
11	Free for peripherals / SCSI / NIC
12	PS2 Mouse
13	FPU / Coprocessor / Inter-processor
14	Primary ATA Hard Disk
15	Secondary ATA Hard Disk

How to initialize the interrupts?

This is a simple method to define an IDT segment

```cpp
void init_idt_desc(u16 select, u32 offset, u16 type,
struct idtdesc *desc)
{
        desc->offset0_15 = (offset & 0xffff);
        desc->select = select;
        desc->type = type;
        desc->offset16_31 = (offset & 0xffff0000) >>
16;
        return;
}
```

And we can now initialize the interupts:

```cpp
#define IDTBASE 0x00000000
#define IDTSIZE 0xFF
idtr kidtr;
```


```cpp
void init_idt(void)
{
        /* Init irq */
        int i;
        for (i = 0; i < IDTSIZE; i++)
                init_idt_desc(0x08, (u32)_asm_schedule,
INTGATE, &kidt[i]); //

        /* Vectors  0 -> 31 are for exceptions */
```

```cpp
        init_idt_desc(0x08, (u32) _asm_exc_GP, INTGATE,
&kidt[13]);              /* #GP */
        init_idt_desc(0x08, (u32) _asm_exc_PF, INTGATE,
&kidt[14]);      /* #PF */

        init_idt_desc(0x08, (u32) _asm_schedule,
INTGATE, &kidt[32]);
        init_idt_desc(0x08, (u32) _asm_int_1, INTGATE,
&kidt[33]);

        init_idt_desc(0x08, (u32) _asm_syscalls,
TRAPGATE, &kidt[48]);
        init_idt_desc(0x08, (u32) _asm_syscalls,
TRAPGATE, &kidt[128]); //48

        kidtr.limite = IDTSIZE * 8;
        kidtr.base = IDTBASE;


        /* Copy the IDT to the memory */
        memcpy((char *) kidtr.base, (char *) kidt,
kidtr.limite);

        /* Load the IDTR registry */
        asm("lidtl (kidtr)");
}
```

After intialization our IDT, we need to activate interrupts by configuring the PIC. The following function will configure the two PICs by writting in their internal registries using the output ports of the processor ```io.outb```. We configure the PICs using the ports:

* Master PIC: 0x20 and 0x21
* Slave PIC: 0xA0 and 0xA1

For a PIC, there is 2 types of registries:

* ICW (Initialization Command Word): reinit the controller
* OCW (Operation Control Word): configure the controller once initialized (used to mask/unmask the interrupts)

```cpp
```

```
void init_pic(void)
{
        /* Initialization of ICW1 */
        io.outb(0x20, 0x11);
        io.outb(0xA0, 0x11);

        /* Initialization of ICW2 */
        io.outb(0x21, 0x20);    /* start vector = 32 */
        io.outb(0xA1, 0x70);    /* start vector = 96 */

        /* Initialization of ICW3 */
        io.outb(0x21, 0x04);
        io.outb(0xA1, 0x02);

        /* Initialization of ICW4 */
        io.outb(0x21, 0x01);
        io.outb(0xA1, 0x01);

        /* mask interrupts */
        io.outb(0x21, 0x0);
        io.outb(0xA1, 0x0);
}
```

PIC ICW configurations details

The registries have to be configured in order.

ICW1 (port 0x20 / port 0xA0)

```
|0|0|0|1|x|0|x|x|
         |   | +--- with ICW4 (1) or without (0)
         |   +----- one controller (1), or cascade (0)
         +--------- triggering by level (level) (1) or
by edge (edge) (0)
```

ICW2 (port 0x21 / port 0xA1)

```
|x|x|x|x|x|0|0|0|
 | | | | |
 +----------------- base address for interrupts vectors
```

ICW2 (port 0x21 / port 0xA1)

For the master:

```
|x|x|x|x|x|x|x|x|
 | | | | | | | |
 +----------------- slave controller connected to the
port yes (1), or no (0)
```

For the slave:
```
|0|0|0|0|0|0|x|x|x|  pour l'esclave
            | | |
            +-------- Slave ID which is equal to the
master port
```

ICW4 (port 0x21 / port 0xA1)

It is used to define in which mode the controller
chould works.

```
|0|0|0|x|x|x|x|1|
       | | | +------ mode "automatic end of interrupt"
AEOI (1)
       | | +-------- mode buffered slave (0) or master
(1)
       | +---------- mode buffered (1)
       +------------ mode "fully nested" (1)
```

Why does idt segments offset are ASM functions?

You should had notice that when I'm initializing our
IDT segments, I'm using offset to segment of code in
Assembly. The se different functions are defined in
[x86int.asm](https://github.com/SamyPesse/How-to-Make-
a-Computer-Operating-
System/blob/master/src/kernel/arch/x86/x86int.asm) and
are following the scheme:

```
%macro  SAVE_REGS 0
        pushad
        push ds
        push es
        push fs
        push gs
```

```
        push ebx
        mov bx,0x10
        mov ds,bx
        pop ebx
%endmacro

%macro   RESTORE_REGS 0
        pop gs
        pop fs
        pop es
        pop ds
        popad
%endmacro

%macro   INTERRUPT 1
global _asm_int_%1
_asm_int_%1:
        SAVE_REGS
        push %1
        call isr_default_int
        pop eax ;;a enlever sinon
        mov al,0x20
        out 0x20,al
        RESTORE_REGS
        iret
%endmacro
```

These macros will be used to define interrupt segment
that will prevent corruption of the different
registries, it will be very usefull for multitasking.

Chapter 8: Memory management: physical and virtual

In the chapter related to the GDT, we saw that using
segmentation a physical memory address is calculated
using a segment selector and an offset.

In this chapter, we are going to implement paging,
paging will translate a linear address from
segmentation into a physical address.

Why do we need paging?

Paging will allow our kernel to:

* use the hard-drive as a memory and not be limited by
the machine ram memory limit

* to have a unique memory space for each process
* to allow and unallow memory space in a dynamic way

In a paged system, each process may execute in its own
4gb area of memory, without any chance of effecting any
other process's memory, or the kernel's. It simplifies
multitasking.

![Processes memories](./processes.png)

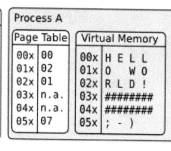

www.ingramcontent.com/pod-product-compliance
Lightning Source LLC
Chambersburg PA
CBHW060937050326
40689CB00013B/3130